MW01515447

UG Says...

Journalist and writer **Arun Babani** has a masters degree in Eastern Philosophy from Mumbai University. He has written a book of spiritual essays titled *Return to Innocence* and two books of poems in Sindhi. His articles have been published in many newspapers and magazines including *Debonair, Weekend* and *DNA*. He lives in Mumbai with his wife and son.

UG Says...

Everyday Thoughts from
UG Krishnamurti

Compiled by **Arun Babani**

Foreword by **Mahesh Bhatt**
Introduction by **Mukunda Rao**

HarperCollins *Publishers* India

Indus Source Books
Indian Spirit, Universal Wisdom

First published in 2009 by Indus Source Books
This edition co-published in India in 2018 by
HarperCollins *Publishers* India
A-75, Sector 57, Noida, Uttar Pradesh 201301, India
www.harpercollins.co.in
and
Indus Source Books
PO Box 6194
Malabar Hill PO
Mumbai 400 006
www.indussource.com

2 4 6 8 10 9 7 5 3 1

Design and Format Copyright © Indus Source 2009, 2018

P-ISBN: 978-93-5302-482-6
E-ISBN: 978-93-5302-483-3

All rights reserved. No part of this publication may be reproduced,
stored in a retrieval system, or transmitted, in any form or by any means,
electronic, mechanical, photocopying, recording or otherwise,
without the prior permission of the publishers.

Printed and bound at
Thomson Press (India) Ltd

This book is produced from independently certified FSC® paper to ensure
responsible forest management.

For my children, Ekant and Prerna

The dearest story book of my life

UG has taught me many valuable things in my life but the most important of them all is contained in two words: Simply Stop.

Imagine the ultimate lightness of being one experiences upon learning the Ultimate Commandment. Years and years spent in *sadhana*, in meditation, in search, simply disappear into thin air and what is left there is the pulse, the beat and the throb of life! Thank you UG, thank you, a million times. In hearing the commandment I simply stopped crawling and became human for the first time in my life.

Foreword

Several years ago, on a fateful night in a colonial house in Yercaud, Tamil Nadu, U.G. Krishnamurti made a bonfire of my friend Chandrasekhar's dreams. He flung audiotapes, video recordings, crammed files containing intimate letters of correspondence written to him by his friends over the years, and hundreds of rare black and white and colour photographs of himself into the fire. As we watched these objects of historical significance, which Chandrasekhar had so painstakingly collected over the years to create a UG archive, go into a blaze, I was reminded of what UG had told me over a cup of coffee in a five star hotel in Mumbai once long ago. 'After I am dead and gone, nothing of me must remain inside of you or outside of you. I can certainly do a lot to see that no establishment or institution of any kind mushrooms around me whilst I am alive. But how do I stop all you guys from enshrining me in your brain?' This unkind act of UG, whom many refer to as the 'raging sage', clearly demonstrated that he was making sure that he kept his promise! Unlike most of us who say something and do totally the opposite, here was a man who was walking his talk. He was erasing his footprints from the sands of time.

But the truth is he has failed to do that. This book is evidence of the irrefutable fact that UG is enshrined in our hearts and he will continue to live there until we drop dead.

Why would he want us to forget him? I wondered to myself. I got an answer to this query a few years later when I called him to wish him on Teachers Day. 'What's your message for mankind on Teacher's Day, UG?' I remember hollering over the overseas phone line, preparing myself for a very subversive answer from the man from whom I have learnt the most important lessons of my life. A brief silence echoed over the phone-static. It was late night in New York and I had pulled UG out of bed. 'All teachers should be destroyed!' he pronounced. 'It is they who are responsible for the mess you find yourselves in. It is the teacher who prevents you from touching your own potential. That is why I say that all models need to be smashed. Life does not imitate, you guys do. And as long as you use a model or follow a teacher you will remain a second hand person. You must have the courage to walk alone. I'm not a teacher and have never been one, but don't you see what a mess the messiahs have left the world in? The world would have been a better place without them . . .' 'Yes, UG,' I whispered, 'thank you and goodbye.' He laughed as he hung up the phone, knowing very well what a shattering impact his words would have on me.

But the truth is that every time I was shattered, in a way I was reborn. Whatever I am today has been shaped by the fierce fights I had with him on the issues of God, life, love, creativity and death. His words are my treasure box from which I pull out gems and share them with the world. Doing that makes me alive. I am happy this book is doing just that.

Mumbai   Mahesh Bhatt
February 2009

A Brief Sketch of U. G. Krishnamurti's Life and Teaching

'I am not a saviour of mankind. I am not in the holy business. I am only interested in describing this state (the natural state), in clearing away the occultation and mystification in which those people in the holy business have shrouded the whole thing. May be I can convince you not to waste a lot of time and energy looking for a state which does not exist except in your imagination.'
~ U. G. Krishnamurti

In the April of 1967 in his 49th year in Paris, persuaded by his friends, U. G. Krishnamurti one day went to a 'girlie show' at Casino de Paris and there all of sudden he felt something strange happening to him. He felt a peculiar movement inside of him and could not make out who was dancing on the floor —he or the dancer. There seemed to be no division between him and the dancer. That marked the beginning of the most astounding and almost incomprehensible mystical experiences you could ever read in the history of mysticism.

They were not the blissful experiences most mystics speak of, but almost a 'physical torture' triggered off by an explosion of energy in his body which eventually put him in what he calls the 'Natural State'.

UG's body began to undergo a tremendous change. In three years the body fell into a new rhythm of its own. The whole chemistry of the body including the five senses was transformed. The eyes stopped blinking, the skin turned soft, when he rubbed any part of his body with his palm, it produced a sort of ash. He developed a breast on the left side. The most phenomenal change of all was that the senses started functioning at their peak sensitivity and the thymus gland, which doctors say is active through childhood until puberty and then becomes dormant, was reactivated.

This was not all. He had visions of Buddha, Jesus, Mahavira, Mohammed, Socrates, of women saints with flowing hair and naked, of the half-lion, half-man god of Hindus, the Greek god with a human body and the body of a seal. And then finally they were all flushed out from his consciousness, for even these sacred images, not to speak of the weird ones of Jungean 'collective consciousness', were all impure in the Natural State and so they had to go. It was a terrible journey and a great sudden leap into the primordial state of consciousness untouched by thought. It was the birth of a New Man!

*

Born in 1918, into an upper-middle class Telugu-speaking Brahmin family, UG was brought up in a religious atmosphere by his grandfather. He learnt to repeat passages from the sacred scriptures, met several holy men who visited his place and found most of them to be hypocrites. He practised meditation and yoga, studied the scriptures and at quite an early age (all this happened between 14 and 21) went through several religious experiences. Yet he was unhappy.

He wanted nothing less than moksha, freedom. At the age of 21, he went to Tiruvannamalai and met the sage Ramana Maharishi. 'Can you give me what you have?' he asked of him. 'Yes,' replied the sage, 'but can you take it?' What was it that Ramana had which he did not, the young seeker wondered as he came out. He had to find it by himself and for himself. He stopped shopping around for gurus and began to explore.

He joined the University of Madras and studied philosophy and psychology, but it gave no answers to his deep questions. One day he asked his professor: 'We are talking about the mind all the time, we are studying so many books, Freud, Jung, Adler and the whole gang. But do you yourself know anything about the mind?' It proved to be not only an embarrassing question but a dangerous one. The practical-minded professor advised him to stop asking such questions and if he wanted to get a degree to merely take down notes, memorise and repeat them in the exams. The student was not interested and dropped out.

Marriage came later. His wife had degrees in English and Sanskrit. Like most men he was a 'dominating husband'. They had four children. By now he had joined the Theosophical Society led by Annie Besant and her close companion C. W. Leadbeater and came in close contact with Jiddu Krishnamurti, who had been proclaimed by Annie Besant as the 'Messiah' of the 20th Century. UG toured the world giving lectures in theosophy though his heart was not in it.

The inevitable happened. The marriage broke up in 1961, he fell out of theosophical society, left JK, and for three years wandered about London 'like a man with no head, blown about like a dry leaf'. This long 'dark night of the soul' ended not in the dawn of not the Upanishadic Bliss or the discovery of 'the space within the heart' but in a 'calamity', an utterly non-religious biological mutation.

*

UG's 'experiences' or what he called the Natural State and his teachings pose a great challenge to the religious traditions all over the world. In fact, there was no teaching. A teaching implies a method or a system, a technique or a new way of thinking to be applied in order to bring about a transformation in our way of life. What UG was saying, he insisted, was outside the field of teachability. In point of fact, there was no teacher, no taught and thereby no teaching. There was no symbolism, no metaphysics, no mysticism involved in his words. He meant what he said, literally. There was nothing new in the language of UG. He did not coin any new words like philosophers and scientists do; he used simple, commonplace words, free of metaphysical overtones and spiritual content, to describe life in pure and simple physical and physiological terms so that it was de-psychologised and demystified, and the implication of what came through is quite revolutionary, to say the least.

Generally, in his freewheeling chats with people all over the world, he did two things:

First, in physical and physiological terms he described the way he, the body, was functioning. He called it the Natural State. It is the state of 'primordial awareness without primitivism', or the 'undivided state of consciousness', where all desires and fear, and the search for happiness and pleasure, God and truth, have come to an end. He insisted that it is not the state of a God-realised man or 'enlightenment'. It is not a state of bliss or supreme happiness either. There is only the throb, the pulse, the beat of life. There thoughts emerge in response to stimuli or a question, and then burn themselves up, releasing energy. There is no soul, no atman, only the body, and the body is immortal. It is an acausal state of 'not-knowing', of wonder. And 'this is the way you,' UG emphasised, 'stripped of the machinations of thought, are also functioning.'

Second, he described the way we function, caught in a world of opposites, constantly struggling to become something other than what we are, and in search of non-existent gods and goals. How we all think and function in a 'thought sphere' just as we all share the same atmosphere for breathing. How and why we have no freedom of action, unless and until thought comes to an end—but then, it is not in the interest of thought to end itself. Thought is self-protective and fascist in nature, and it will use every trick under the sun to give momentum to its own continuity. Thought controls, moulds, and shapes our ideas and actions. Idea and action—they are one and the same. All our actions are born out of ideas. Our ideas are thoughts passed on to us from generation to generation. And this thought is not the instrument to help us to live in harmony with the life around us. That is why we create all these ecological problems, problems of pollution, and the problem of possibly destroying ourselves with the most destructive weapons that we have invented.

*

UG died on 22 March 2007 at the age of eighty-nine in Vallecrosia, Italy, at the villa of a friend. UG never showed any fear or concern about dying, insisting that 'life and death cannot be separated . . . when what you call clinical death takes place, the body breaks itself into its constituent elements and that provides the basis for the continuity of life . . . in that sense the body is immortal.'

The effect that he has had, and will continue to have, on legions of his admirers is difficult to put into words. With his flowing silvery hair, deep-set eyes and elongated Buddha-like ears he was an explosive yet cleansing presence.

February 200   Mukunda Rao

Preface

Spirituality is a multimillion dollar industry today, growing in leaps, with ever new gurus,masters,methods and techniques being born every other day, with each claiming to be the straight, quick road to instant nirvana, moksha, enlightenment. I can't say whether this news is good, bad or ugly. All I can fathom from the face of the society is that all this talk of truth and reality doesn't seem to operate in the daily lives of these dreamers. These spiritual goodies don't seem to make any difference to the violence and greed in people's lives.

UG on the other hand stands alone in this whole mess and declares, 'I have nothing to sell, no point to prove, no axe to grind', because, as he says, 'you are chasing a shadow, what you want simply doesn't exist.'

I believe one has to get into the muck to be able to do the cleaning. The chaos of questions is a step towards the order of complete peace with oneself. So if you have gone through the sorrows of seeking and searching, with this book you might finally arrive at not finding the answers, but with some luck, at dropping the questions!

4 February 2009   A.B.

Thought
is
your enemy.

*Not knowing is
your natural state.*

Flush out
your past
from your system.

Be in unfrightened
self-abandonment.

Be in uncomplaining self-reliance.

Give up. Simply stop.
Stop searching.

De-psychologise and de-spiritualise yourself.

Have the courage
to stand alone.

*Life is a movement
without direction,
a passion that burns
without purpose.*

As long as you use your thoughts to understand anything, you are not in contact with anything living.

*Life is a
unitary process.*

Things and thoughts are disjointed in each moment.

Every time
a thought
is born,
you are born.

Thoughts
arise from
wants.

Happiness without unhappiness is unnatural.

Anyone who wants more than the basic needs of food, clothing and shelter is basically neurotic.

Maya means
to measure everything
from one´s own
point of view.

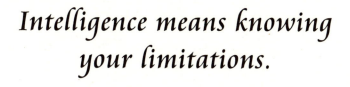

Intelligence means knowing your limitations.

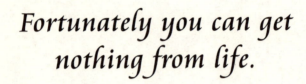

Fortunately you can get nothing from life.

You are always
suffering
because you
want to be
other than
what you are.

The so called self realisation
is the discovery
for yourself
and by yourself
that there is
no self to discover.

The fundamental attributes of life are survival and reproduction.

Nature is busy creating absolutely unique individuals, whereas culture has invented a single mould to which all must conform. It is grotesque.

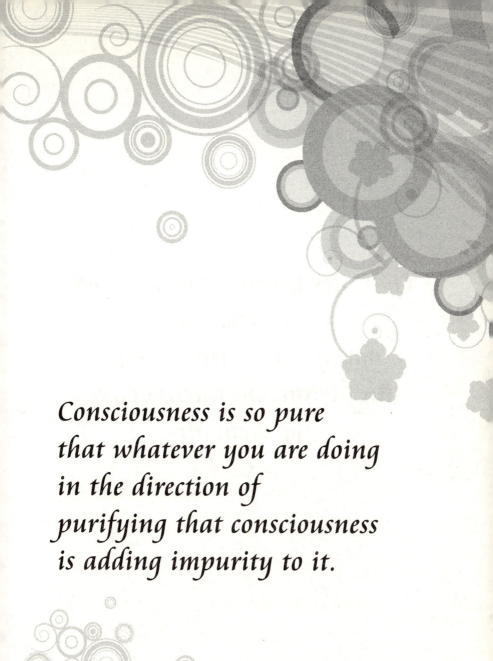

Consciousness is so pure that whatever you are doing in the direction of purifying that consciousness is adding impurity to it.

That messy thing called 'mind'
has created
many destructive things.
By far the most destructive
of them all
is God.

*Only if you reject
all the other paths,
can you discover
your own.*

When you know nothing,
you say a lot.
When you know something,
what is there to say?

The only way for anyone interested in finding out what this is all about is to watch how this separation is occuring, how you are separating yourself from the things that are happening around you and inside you.

It is the most difficult thing
to be an ordinary person.

The peak of sex experience
is the one thing in life you have
that comes close to being
a first hand experience.
    All the rest of your experiences
are second hand, somebody else's.

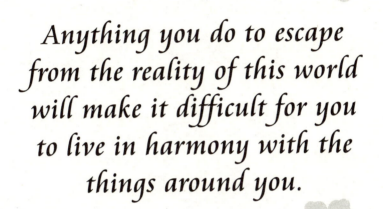

Anything you do to escape from the reality of this world will make it difficult for you to live in harmony with the things around you.

The understanding is the
absence of the demand for
understanding.

To be yourself
is very easy,
you don't have to do
a thing.

Everything you are doing to be at peace with yourself is what is destroying the peace that is already there.

You think the thoughts
of your society, feel
the feelings of your
society and experience
the experience of your
society. There is no
new experience.

*Knowing
what is there
is impossible.*

To acquire more and more knowledge is to acquire more and more power over others.

In order to bring doing to an end, you are doing something else. That is the crux of the problem.

All our problems have
arisen because of
our acceptance that
it is possible for us to
understand the reality
of the world or existence.

Your value system is responsible for the human tragedy, forcing everybody to fit into that model.

Wanting and thinking always go together.

The hope keeps
you going.

If you are lucky,
you are lucky,
that's all.

Culture demands that you should be something other than what you are. What a tremendous amount of energy we waste trying to become that. But if that energy is released, living becomes very simple. Then what is it that you cannot do?

You have to actually touch life at a point where nobody has touched it before. Nobody can teach you that.

Your search for happiness
is prolonging
your unhappiness.

There is no such
thing as looking at
something without
the interference
of knowledge.

*You have invented
the goal
to give yourself hope.*

*If you are lucky enough
to be free from fear
then there is no God.*

Perfection and absolutes
are false.

How to live one's life is
the one question which has
transformed itself into
millions of questions.

A real guru,
if there is one,
frees you from himself.

You don't stop searching
because such an act would be
the end of you.

*You are lost only because
you are searching.*

Knowledge is just naming things.

*Your insecurity springs
from your refusal to face the
temporary nature of thought.*

I am trying to stop
what you are making
out of what I am saying.

Spirituality is the invention of the mind, and the mind is a myth.

The moment you ask 'how',
you turn to some one
for answers,
becoming dependent.

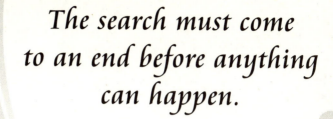

*The search must come
to an end before anything
can happen.*

You can never hear one word from anyone no matter how intimately you think you are in relationship with that person. You hear only your own translations always.

Because you are
not interested in
the everyday things
and happenings
around you, you
have invented the
beyond, timelessness,
God, truth, reality,
enlightenment
or whatever, and
search for it.

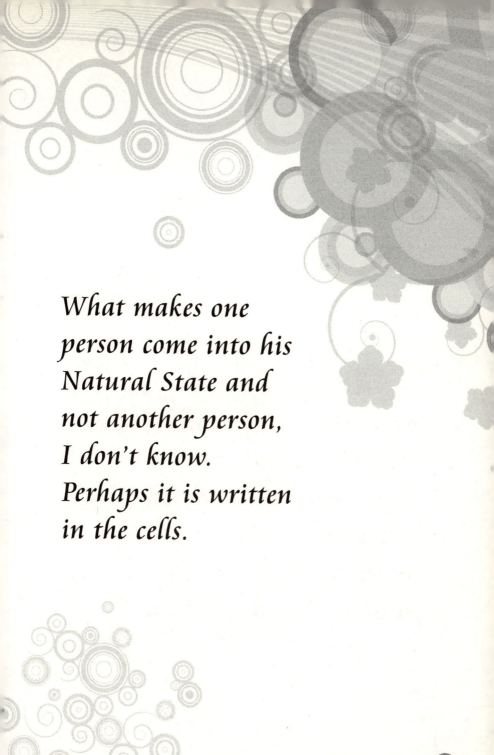

What makes one
person come into his
Natural State and
not another person,
I don't know.
Perhaps it is written
in the cells.

No dialogue is possible.
When the you is not
there, when the question
is not there, what is, is
understanding. You are
finished. You'll walk out.

To be yourself requires extraordinary intelligence. You are blessed with that intelligence. Nobody need give it to you. Nobody can take it away from you. He who lets that express itself in its own way is a natural man.

Man becomes man for the first time when he frees himself from the burden of heritage of man as a whole.

Animals follow.
Animals create leaders.
And animal traits are
still persisting in man.
That is why he creates
a leader and follows.

Your naturalness is something that you don't have to know. You just have to let that function in its own way.

You become restless
because of this drive in
you which is put in there
by the society or culture
that makes you feel
that there is something
more interesting,
more meaningful,
more purposeful, than
whatever you are doing
this moment.

The hunger must burn itself out completely without knowing satisfaction. The thirst you have must burn itself out without being quenched.

Wanting to change your material life into that so-called religious pattern given to you by these religious people is destroying the possibility of your living in harmony and accepting the reality of this material world exactly the way it is.

Any doing in any direction is violence. Any effort is violence. Anything you do with thought to create a peaceful state of mind is using force and so is violence.

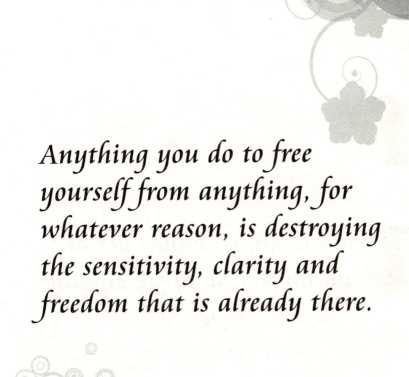

Anything you do to free yourself from anything, for whatever reason, is destroying the sensitivity, clarity and freedom that is already there.

Seeing today demands action.
Seeing tomorrow involves only
hope.

The energy you are devoting to the search is taking away the energy you need to live.

*Getting what
you want
in this world
is a relatively
easy thing
if you are
ruthless enough.*

You can't come into your own
uniqueness unless the whole of
human experience
is thrown out of your system.
Then you are on your own.

The body, which is only interested in survival and procreation, treats both pain and pleasure alike. It is you who insist on stopping pain and extending pleasure.

*I don't know
what happiness is
and so
I never would be
unhappy.*

How does the body turn over many times during sleep without your being aware of it, much less trying to control it? The body is handling itself.

When you see for
yourself the absurdity
of your search, the whole
culture is reduced to
ashes inside you and
then you are out of that.

Questioning is not a hallmark of intelligence. Cessation of questioning is.

All the accumulated knowledge, experience and suffering of mankind is inside of you. You must build a huge bonfire within you. Then you will become an individual. There is no other way.

You were born and are alive because your parents had sex, period. Don't look for a meaning to life.

The way you are thinking, feeling and experiencing is exactly the same way everyone else in this world is thinking, feeling and experiencing.

*It is the object
that creates
the subject.*

The cultural input, or what society has placed before us as the goal for all of us to reach and attain, is the enemy of this living organism.

Happiness is a
cultural input.
Is there any
such thing as
happiness?
I would say, no.

Nothing needs to be done to change anything. Things are changing in their own ways.

When you are no longer caught up in the dichotomy of right and wrong, or good and bad, you can never do anything wrong. As long as you are caught up in this duality, the danger is that you will always be wrong.

*Not answers
but ending of questions
is the important thing.*

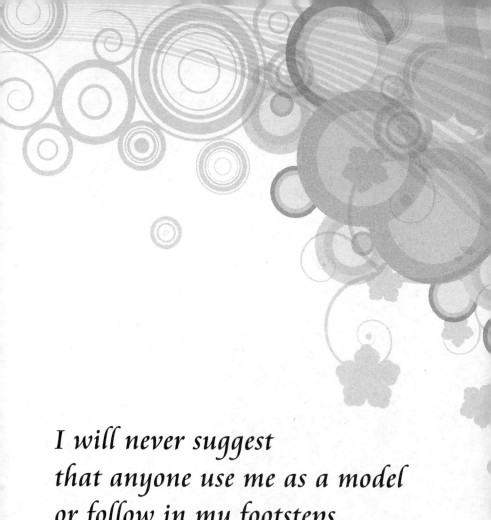

*I will never suggest
that anyone use me as a model
or follow in my footsteps.*

Man has created religion because it gives him a cover.

An artist is a craftsman
like any other craftsman.
He uses that tool
to express himself.
All art is a
sensual movement.

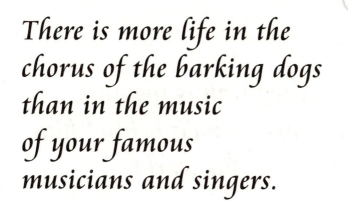

There is more life in the
chorus of the barking dogs
than in the music
of your famous
musicians and singers.

*A messiah is the one
who leaves a mess behind him
in this world.*

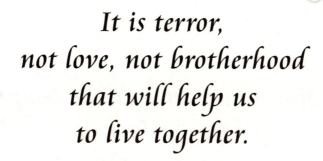

It is terror,
not love, not brotherhood
that will help us
to live together.

Going to the pub or the temple
is exactly the same;
it is a quick fix.

God and sex go together.
If God goes sex goes too.

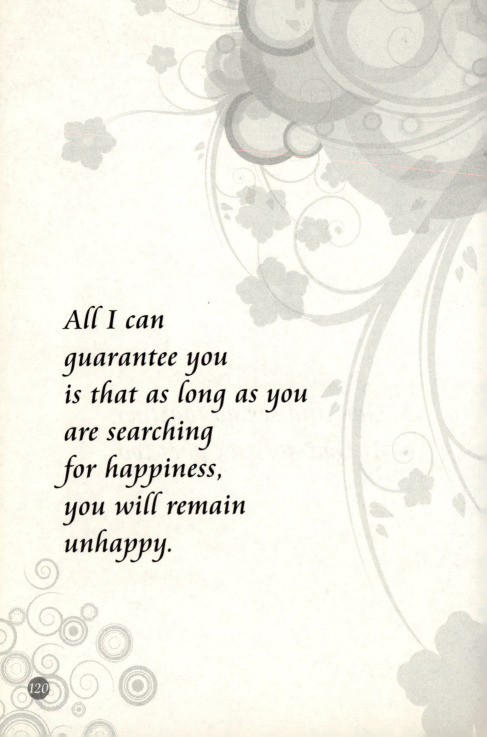

All I can
guarantee you
is that as long as you
are searching
for happiness,
you will remain
unhappy.

Understanding yourself is one of the greatest jokes perpetrated not only by the purveyors of ancient wisdom-the holy men-but also the modern scientists. The psychologists love to talk about self knowledge, self actualisation, living from moment to moment and such rot.

Humility is an art that one practises. There is no such thing as humility. As long as you know, there is no humility. The known and humility cannot coexist.

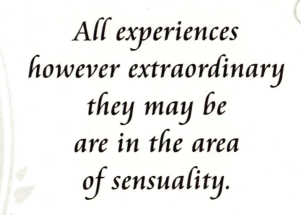

*All experiences
however extraordinary
they may be
are in the area
of sensuality.*

Love and hate are opposite ends
of the same spectrum.
They are one and the same thing.
They are much closer
than kissing cousins.

There is nobody like you anywhere in this world among the six billion people we have. The individual is an extraordinary piece of creation by the evolutionary process.

Gurus play a social role,
so do prostitutes.

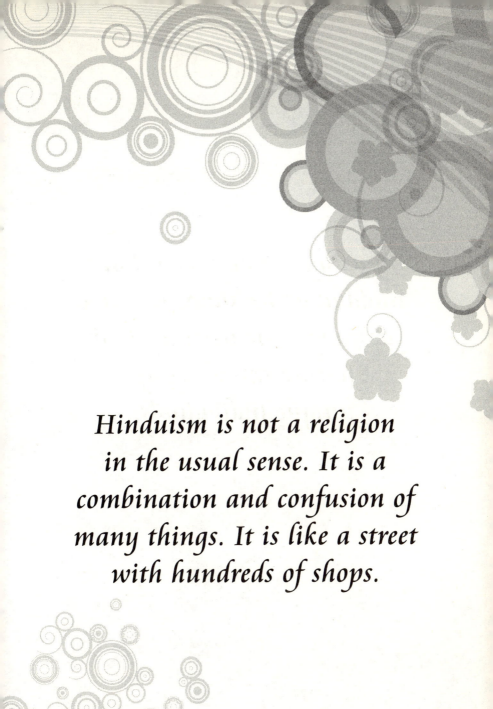

Hinduism is not a religion in the usual sense. It is a combination and confusion of many things. It is like a street with hundreds of shops.

By using the models of Jesus, Buddha or Krishna, we have destroyed the possibility of nature throwing up unique individuals.

The man who spoke of
'Love thy neighbor as
thyself' is responsible
for this horror
in the world today.

The appreciation of music, poetry and the arts is all culturally determined and is the product of thought. It is acquired taste that tells you that Beethoven's ninth symphony is more beautiful than a chorus of cats screaming; both produce equally valid sensations.

We are no more
purposeful or meaningful
than any other thing
on this planet. We are not
created for any grander
purpose than the ants that
are there or the flies that
are hovering around us,
or the mosquitoes
that are sucking
our blood.

We have to accept the absurdity
of depending upon anything.
We must face our helplessness.

You think that through a
self imposed asceticism you
will increase your awareness
and then be able to use that
awareness to be happy.
No chance.

You must be a machine, function automatically in this world, never questioning your actions before, during or after they occur.

Society is not going to feed you unless you give something in return. You have to give them what they want, not what you have to give.

When hoping
and attempting
to understand is
not there then
life becomes
meaningful.

What I am suggesting is
that the very demand
to understand
the mystery of existence
is destructive.
Just leave the mystery alone.

Ambition is a reality,
competition is a reality,
but you have superimposed on
that reality the idea that you
should not be ambitious.
It has turned us all into
neurotic individuals.

We demand that there must be something permanent. That is what these religious teachers are peddling. They offer you eternal happiness.

The intelligence that is necessary for survival is already there in the physical organism, you don't have to learn a thing.

There are moments of happiness and there are moments of unhappiness. But the demand to be in a permanent state of happiness is the enemy of this body.

The mind has invented
both religion and dynamite
to protect what it regards
as its best interests.

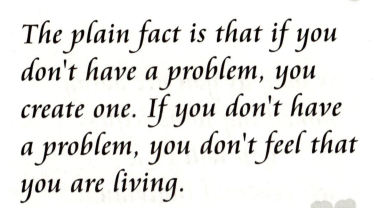

The plain fact is that if you don't have a problem, you create one. If you don't have a problem, you don't feel that you are living.

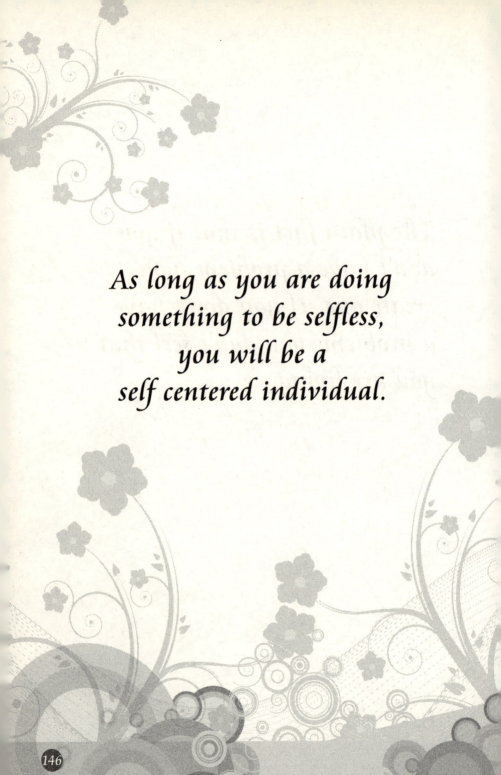

As long as you are doing
something to be selfless,
you will be a
self centered individual.

Truth is a movement.
You can't capture it,
contain it,
give expression to it
or use it to
advance your interests.

A natural man is of no use to society. On the contrary, he becomes a threat.

Something is trying
to express itself
and the culture
is pushing it down.
When once it throws
the culture out
then it expresses itself
in its own way.

This consciousness which is functioning in me, in you, is the same. In me it has no frontiers. In you there are frontiers. You are enclosed in that.

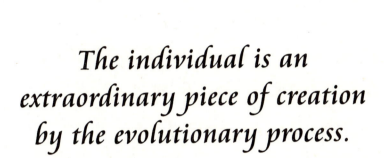

The individual is an
extraordinary piece of creation
by the evolutionary process.

You are not an ordinary being.
You are an extraordinary being.
The ideal of perfection
that has been placed before us
has put the whole thing
on the wrong track.
The perfect being
doesn't exist at all.

Thought is only
for the purposes of
communication.
Otherwise it has no
value whatever.

Life guides you. This organism
is interested in protecting itself
and it knows how to survive.
Just use your eyes
and your ears
and they will
guide you.

These religious
people have created a
policeman inside you.
That hasn't helped you
in any way.

You don't know what is good.
You know only
what is good for you.
That's all you are interested in.
All your art and reason
centers around that.

A moral man is
a frightened man,
a chicken hearted man.
That is why
he practices morality
and sits in judgment
over others.

If you don't recognise
what you are looking at,
it means you are not there.

A sage cannot have a follower because it is not an experience that can be shared. Even an ordinary experience you can't share with others. Can you tell somebody who has never experienced sex what the sex experience is like?

The absence of imagination, the absence of will, the absence of effort, the absence of all movement in any direction, on any level, in any dimension— that is the thing.

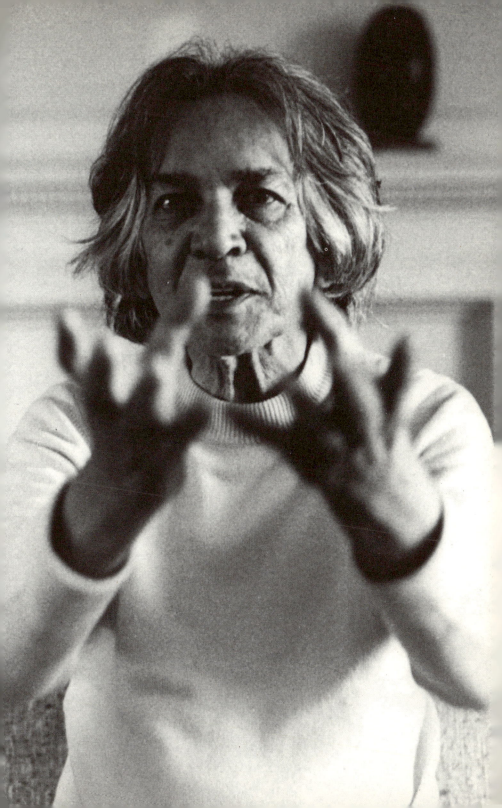

We have placed before man the ideal of a perfect man, a truly religious man. So anything you do to reach that goal of perfection is destroying the sensitivity of this body.

That is real courage—the courage to brush aside everything that man has experienced and felt before you.

If you are lucky enough to be free from this pursuit of virtue as a goal, along with it the vice also goes out of your system.

If you and I go, life goes on. Those lights go off but the electricity continues.

What is truth for me
is something that cannot,
under any circumstances,
be communicated to you.
The certainity here cannot
be transmitted to another.
For this reason
the whole guru business
is absolute nonsense.

I don't believe in education.
You can teach a technique—
mathematics, automechanics,
but not integrity. How can you
teach them about non-greed
and non-ambition in an
insanely greedy and ambitious
society? You will only succeed
in making them more neurotic.

The saints and saviours have only succeeded in setting you adrift in life with pain and misery and the restless feeling that there must be something more meaningful or interesting to do with one's life.

Only technology progresses, while we as a race are moving closer to complete destruction of ourselves and the world.

Violence is an integral part of the evolutionary process. That violence is essential for the survival of the living organism. You can't condemn the hydrogen bomb, for it is an extension of the policeman and your desire to be protected.

What I am trying to say is that you must discover something for yourself. But do not be misled into thinking that what you find will be of use to society, that it can be used to change the world. You are finished with society, that is all.

God is the ultimate pleasure,
uninterrupted happiness.
No such thing exists.
Transformation, moksha,
liberation and all that stuff
are just variations on the same
theme: permanent happiness.

There is one thought.
Everything exists in
relationship to that one
thought. That thought is 'me'.
Anything you experience
based on that thought
is an illusion.

There is no such thing as your mind and my mind. There is only MIND—the totality of all that has been known, felt and experienced by man, and handed down from generation to generation.

What I am emphasising is that we are trying to solve our basic human problems through a psychological framework, when actually the problem is neurological. The body is involved.

Where is this ego or
self that you talk of?
Your non-existent self has heard
of spirituality and bliss
from some one.

To experience this thing called
bliss you feel you must control
your thoughts. It is impossible,
you will burn yourself and die
if you attempt it.

The day man experienced that self consciousness that made him feel separate and superior to the other animals, at that moment he began sowing the seeds of his own destruction.

*All I am saying
is that the peak
you are seeking is
already inside you,
in the harmonious
functioning
of the body.*

I am not an alarmist. I am not frightened, I am not interested in saving the world. Mankind is doomed any way.

Unless you are free from the desire of all desires, moksha, liberation or self-realisation, you will be miserable. The ultimate goal—which society has placed before us—is the one that has to go.

Effortlessness through effort is like peace through war.

Courage is not
an instrument or quality
you can use
to get somewhere.
The stopping of doing
is courage.
The ending of tradition
in you is courage.

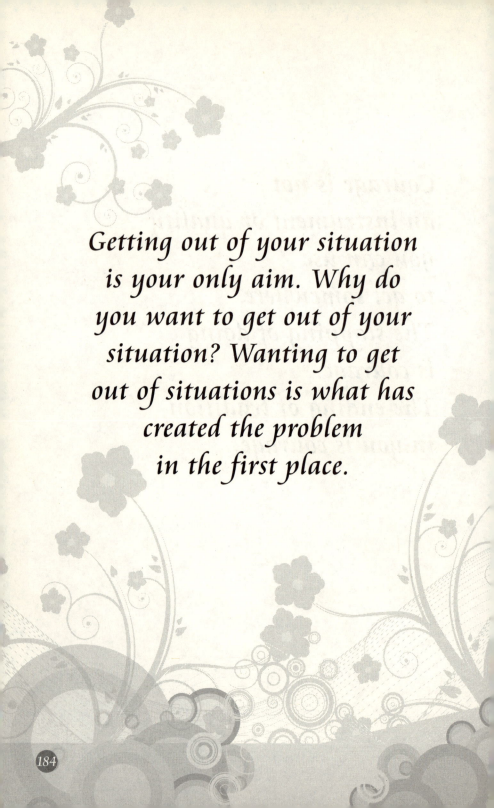

Getting out of your situation is your only aim. Why do you want to get out of your situation? Wanting to get out of situations is what has created the problem in the first place.

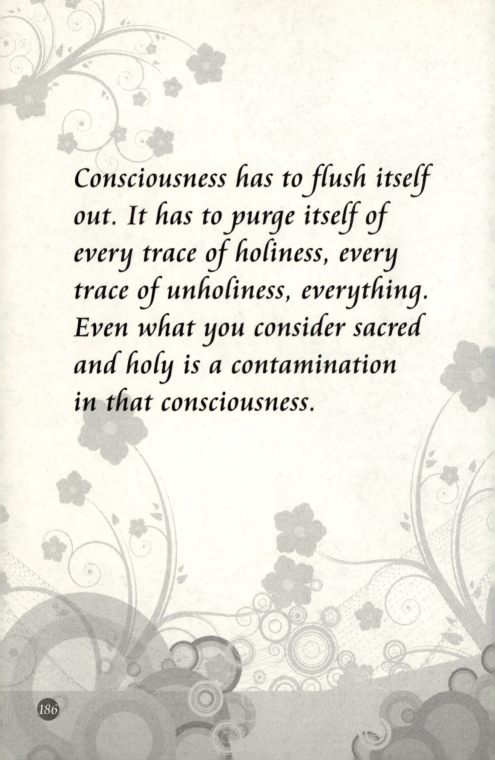

Consciousness has to flush itself out. It has to purge itself of every trace of holiness, every trace of unholiness, everything. Even what you consider sacred and holy is a contamination in that consciousness.

I have no teaching. There is nothing to preserve. Teaching implies something that can be used to bring about change. Sorry, there is no teaching here, just disjointed, disconnected sentences.

As long as you think,
accept and believe
that there is something
to understand,
demanding search
and struggle,
you are lost
and will live in misery.

Anything you try to make
out of my statements is not it.
You sense a freshness, a living
quality to what is being
said here. That is so,
but this cannot be used
for anything.
It is worthless.

My mission, if there is any, is to debunk every statement that I have ever made. If you take seriously and try to use or apply what I have said you will be in danger.

The only answer to
this human problem
is not to be found
through new ideas,
new concepts or
new ideologies, but
through bringing
about a change in
the chemistry of the
human body.

Whatever you do in the pursuit
of truth or reality
takes you away from your own
very natural state
in which you always are.

To deny yourself
the basic needs
is not a sign of spirituality.
But to require more than
food, clothing and shelter
is a neurotic state of mind.

You are dissatisfied with your everyday experiences and so you want new ones. You want to perfect yourself, to change yourself. You are trying to be something other than what you are. It is this that is taking you away from yourself.

This movement of thought within you is parallel to the movement of life but isolated from it. It can never touch life. You are a living creature yet you lead your entire life within the realm this isolated, parallel movement of thought. You cut yourself off from life.

The natural state is not a thoughtless state. You will never be without thought. Being able to think is necessary to survive but in this state thought stops choking you. It falls into its natural rhythm.

If it had not been for culture, life would have produced more flowers, different kinds and variety of flowers, not only the one rose that you are so proud of. You want to turn everything into one model. What for?

When this thing happened to me I realised that all my search was in the wrong direction and that this is not something religious, not something psychological, but a purely physiological functioning of the senses at their peak capacities.

For some reason or the other
the culture has limited the
possibility of the potential
evolving into its completeness
and wholeness.

Life is trying to destroy the enclosing thing, that dead structure of thought and experience which is not of its nature. Its trying to come out, to break open.
You don't want that.

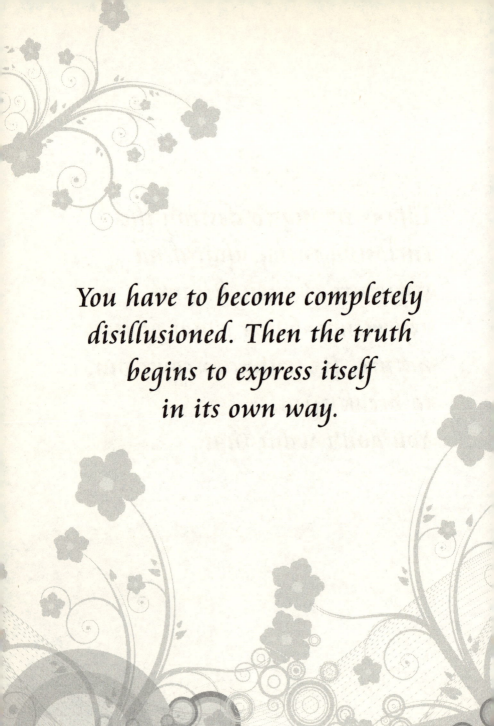

You have to become completely
disillusioned. Then the truth
begins to express itself
in its own way.

202

The separation between mind and body must come to an end. Actually, there is no separation. I have no objection to the word mind but it is not in one particular location or area. Every cell in your system has a mind of its own.

What separates you, what isolates you, is thought. It creates frontiers, boundaries. Once that is not there you are boundless, limitless.

In a way the whole
of life is like a great
big dream. I am looking
at you but I really don't
know anything about
you. This is a dream,
a dream world. There
is no reality to it at all.

Look here, there is no
present to the structure
of the you. All that is
there is the past which
is trying to project
itself into the future.

You arrive seeking understanding, while I am only interested in making it clear that there is nothing to understand.

It is thought that has created the reality of the body, of your living, of your sleep, and of all your perceptions. You experience this reality through knowledge. Otherwise there is no way of your knowing for yourself that you have a body, that you are alive, that you are awake. All that is knowledge.

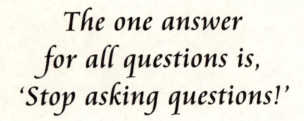

The one answer
for all questions is,
'Stop asking questions!'